Where's My Miracle?

Joni Eareckson Tada

ROSE PUBLISHING/ASPIRE PRESS

Torrance, California

Where's My Miracle?
© Copyright 2015 Joni Eareckson Tada

Aspire Press, an imprint
of Rose Publishing, Inc.
4733 Torrance Blvd., #259
Torrance, California 90503 USA
www.rose-publishing.com
www.aspirepress.com

Printed by Regent Publishing Services Ltd.
Printed in China
November 2014, 1st printing

Contents

The Author

Joni Eareckson Tada, the founder and chief executive officer of Joni and Friends International Disability Center, is an international advocate for people with disabilities. A diving accident in 1967 left Joni Eareckson, then 17,  a quadriplegic in a wheelchair. After two years of rehabilitation, she emerged with new skills and a fresh determination to help others in similar situations. She founded Joni and Friends in 1979 to provide Christ-centered programs to special needs families, as well as training to churches. Through the organization's *Christian Institute on Disability*, Joni and her team have helped develop disability ministry courses of study in major Christian universities and seminaries. Visit us at www.joniandfriends.org.

Joni's Story

Nothing can describe the horror when you hear doctors say, "You will never walk or use your hands again." All I could pray was, "Oh God, may it not be so!" Visitors were a highlight—they brightened the otherwise dreary days. One afternoon, a man I had seen in the hospital hallways entered my four-bed ward. He came directly to my Stryker frame where I lay, paralyzed.

I liked his friendly, open face. He talked freely about God and asked about my life before the accident. "Joni," he said, "today is the day you're going to begin your healing." I knew my faith was weak, but the Bible verses he shared increased my faith. He prayed, anointed me with oil, and we believed together that God would heal me. But nothing happened. When a month passed, I thought, *Maybe my healing will happen gradually.* But my fingers and feet never got the message: *Move, in Jesus' name, move!*

When I was released from the hospital, friends took me to healing crusades. I searched my heart for unconfessed sin. My faith was so strong, I called people to say, "I'll be running up your sidewalk soon!" Still, I remained paralyzed. Either God was playing some kind of cruel joke on me or my view of Scripture was wrong. But I couldn't imagine a God who expected his children to jump through so many hoops, and cruel tricks aren't a part of his character. So what's the story?

My Convictions

After decades of reading and researching the Bible, I've come to this conclusion: God certainly can, and sometimes does, heal people in a miraculous way today. But the Bible does not teach that he will always heal those who come to him in faith. God reserves the right to heal or not to heal as he sees fit.

To understand how I reached this conclusion, ask yourself this question: "Just what is disease?" I don't mean what is it medically or what is its physical cause; I mean what is it biblically? Why is it here? What is its purpose? The answers to these questions will shed a lot of light on the subject of healing. And to find the answers we need to go all the way back to the garden of Eden.

Death, Disease, and Promised Healing

Mankind's rebellion against God resulted in death. Disease, sickness, and disaster are simply part of the package that goes with death. Every human being as well as all of nature is under this curse. But God did not abandon mankind. God promised that one day the Messiah would come to reverse the curse over the earth, and rescue those who would place their trust in him (Gen. 3:15–19; Isa. 53:4–6).

When the Messiah comes, he will deal with sin.

He will do this by forgiving the sins of God's people and by judging those who ultimately refuse to obey God (Mic. 5:2–5; Isa. 9:6–7).

The Messiah will deal with sin's results.

The world of nature will be restored; the physical earth and animals will be affected; the sorrow and frustrations of mankind will be erased; and as for disease, God will cause the eyes of the blind to be opened, the ears of the deaf unstopped, and the lame to leap like a deer (see Isa. 35:5–9; 65:25).

With promises like these, the air of expectation for the Messiah's coming was at a fever pitch by Jesus' day. But God's people thought that everything the Messiah was to do would be accomplished in a single coming. *They did not understand that their*

King would come first in humility as a servant, and only later in all his regal splendor (during which time he would complete all the promises and usher in a new earth where disease and death would be banished, and peace and joy would reign).

Healing: Launching Jesus' Kingdom

The kingdom of God was launched with the coming of Christ, though its fullness was still to be in the future (see Matt. 6:10; 25:31–34; Mark 14:25; Gal. 5:21; 2 Thess. 1:5; Rev. 11:15). Jesus had come to challenge Satan's false claim as ruler of the earth and to establish his own kingship, claiming back what was rightfully his. He had come to begin to reverse the curse—he had come to deal with sin and its results.

How did Jesus deal with sin?

Jesus came to pay sin's penalty on the cross, releasing believers from its power to harm them eternally. But to this day, Christians still struggle against sin (we won't be able to perfectly obey until the kingdom comes in its fullness). Yes, he broke the power of sin, but (and this is the important part) he didn't remove its *presence* from us.

How did Jesus deal with sin's results?

He demonstrated that he truly had the power to reverse the effects of sin: Finding disease, he healed the sick. Faced with demon possession, he cast out spirits. Threatened by storms, he quieted the waves to demonstrate his kingship over nature. He was showing that he was retaking the rule of earth for himself.

But to this day, people still get sick and die; and there are still catastrophes of nature. Yes, he calmed the stormy sea, but hurricanes still take their toll. And though Jesus raised the dead, even Lazarus eventually ended up in a grave. Yes, Jesus healed many who had diseases, but what about the thousands in Israel who never met Jesus to be cured by him?

Jesus' plan was to begin the kingdom and lay its foundation at his first coming. He wanted to give a foreshadowing of what things would be like at the end of time when the kingdom of God would be complete! Christians are living in two ages at once—we experience the trials, temptations, and problems of this age, even though we have tasted the powers of the age to come. God is King right now, but he doesn't always flex "his kingly muscles." Rather than totally wiping out sin and its results, he gives Christians a taste or down payment of what the kingdom and its fullness will be like.

A Kingdom View Toward Healing

Jesus' miracles, including healing, didn't guarantee the end of any of sin's results for those who follow him. And so, in this age, we still must put up with storms, abuse from wicked people, death, and yes, disease: whether spinal cord injury or multiple sclerosis, autism, or Alzheimers.

So does God want us to pray for healing? Yes! The Bible tells us to pray for healing (James 5:14).

Should we fully expect God to heal? All healing from every sort of affliction always comes from his hand (Ps. 103:3). But in view of the fact that the kingdom has not yet come in its fullness, we are not to automatically expect it. Why should we arbitrarily single out disease—which is just one of sin's many results—and treat it in a special way as something that Christians shouldn't have to put up with? We are living in "this present age" and the emphasis on earthly problems in the New Testament tells us we're going to have to put up with plenty! (Mark 10:30; Eph. 1:21).

Does it show a lack of faith if people are not healed? No! The focus of our faith should *always* be Jesus. And although Jesus wants what's best for his followers, that doesn't mean best is an easy life with no head colds or back pain; God's idea of best may be physical hardships that drive us closer to him.

Why does God heal some people and not others? We cannot know what God has not revealed. God may occasionally grant miraculous healing as a gracious glimpse, a sneak preview, of the coming age. So when people are healed miraculously, it should encourage us to look forward to the time when healing will be for *everyone*.

What should be our response when God doesn't heal us?

When bedsores afflict me as boils did Job, I will say with him, "Shall we accept good from God, and not trouble?" (Job 2:10). And when I feel bound to my wheelchair as Paul was to his chains, I will say with him, "For it has been granted to you on behalf of Christ not only to believe on him, but also to suffer for him" (Phil. 1:29).

The King Is Coming Back

What should be our response as we wait for the completed kingdom and healing for all? The apostle Paul wrote, "We ourselves, who have the firstfruits of the Spirit, groan inwardly as we wait eagerly for… the redemption of our bodies. For in this hope we were saved. But hope that is seen is no hope at all. Who hopes for what he already has? But if we hope for what we do not yet have, we wait for it patiently" (Rom. 8:23–25).

Shouldn't We Expect Miraculous Healing?

Christians seeking healing often use the following arguments:

Jesus Christ is "the same yesterday, today, and forever." Because he healed all who came to him in faith in the gospels, he will do the same today.

The mistake in this line of reasoning comes from failing to distinguish between *who God is* and *what he does.* Who he is never changes, but what he does often will. God's character and attributes are the things about him that cannot change, but what he does

is always changing: at one time God acted through the nation of Israel; now he acts through his church.

At one time Jesus submitted to those who mocked him; someday he will take vengeance on his enemies. Just because God acted one way toward his people in the Old Testament doesn't force him to deal with us in the same way (if this were not so, our shoes would not wear out as they did on the feet of the Israelites wandering in the desert). Jesus *is* the same... but the way he deals with us is not.

Miracles were not confined only to the days of Christ and his apostles—the age of miracles is still with us.

The mistake in this line of reasoning is a failure to understand the purpose of miracles in the New Testament. Miracles had a special place *for the time of Christ* because they proved who he was and who he claimed to be—the Promised One of Israel. Miracles had a special place *for the time of the apostles* because they proved that the apostles, too, were who they claimed to be—Christ's specially chosen men to get the wobbly-kneed, newborn church on its feet. There was no New Testament at the time of the apostles—the Holy Spirit gave these special leaders prophecies and revelations to fill in as stopgaps until the full New Testament message could be written down.

Do Bible Promises Guarantee Healing?

Christians who seek healing lean on the following key passages:

- "This is the confidence we have in approaching God: that if we ask anything according to his will, he hears us. And if we know that he hears us—whatever we ask—we know that we have what we ask of him" (1 John 5:14–15).

- "But those who hope in the Lord will renew their strength. They will soar on wings like eagles; they will run and not grow weary, they will walk and not faint" (Isa. 40:31).

- "You hear, O Lord, the desire of the afflicted; you encourage them, and you listen to their cry" (Ps. 10:17).

- "Is any one of you sick? He should call the elders of the church to pray over him and anoint him with oil in the name of the Lord. And the prayer offered in faith will make the sick person well; the Lord will raise him up..." (James 5:14–15).

- "He said to the paralytic, 'I tell you, get up, take your mat and go home.' He got up, took his mat and walked out in full view of them all. This amazed everyone and they praised God, saying, 'We have never seen anything like this!'" (Mark 2:11–12).

These are staggering promises, but when Christians don't get their prayers answered the way they hoped (that is, when God's answer is "no"), what are we to do with verses like these?

God guarantees answers to prayer, but his answers depend on whether or not *our requests fall in line with his will.*

Jesus said in John 15:7, *"If you remain in me and my words remain in you,* ask whatever you wish, and it will be given you." Jesus' words imply a consistent lifestyle of obedience and closeness with him, not a sporadic spirituality. Many Christians have a God-exists-to-make-me-happy mentality that can carry over into their prayer life. But what if you are a godly Christian who is remaining in Christ and his Word, yet you are still sick? Well, if you have tried everything to be healed but nothing has changed, then has it occurred to you that the reason you are in your present condition is that God, in his wisdom, purposes that your condition be allowed to remain?

Praying
"If It Be Thy Will"

Some people say, *If we don't expect God to heal us, then he won't! Ending a prayer for healing with the words "If it be thy will" actually shows a lack of faith. Shouldn't we strive to reach the place where we are so in touch with God that we can understand what he wills in every case and then pray with full faith and assurance?*

Friend, if the authors of the New Testament did not claim to always know God's mind, who are we to think *we* can? God is so above us, and his ways are so unlike ours: "Oh, the depth of the riches of the wisdom and knowledge of God! How unsearchable his judgments, and his paths beyond tracing out! 'Who has known the mind of the Lord? Or who has been his counselor?'" (Rom. 11:33–34).

Our attitude should reflect James 4:15, "If it is the Lord's will, we will live and do this or that." Once when Paul was asked by some Christians to stay in Ephesus to help them, he did not pretend to be able to read God's mind to somehow discern his will. He merely said, "I will come back if it is God's will" (Acts 18:21). Because we are humans, it is so easy for us to make mistakes and misread God's will, especially when we earnestly desire to be healthy and not sick. It takes real humility and self-denial to put our pleas for healing before God and then willingly leave the answer with him.

How Could It Be God's Will to Deny a Christian's Request for Healing?

If God chooses not to heal an individual, his reasons are good. The pages of Scripture teem with good things that can come from suffering.

- Pain and discomfort get our minds off the temporary things of this world and force us to think about God (2 Cor. 4:16–18).

- Suffering drives us into his Word more than usual (Ps. 119:71).

- Trials knock us off our proud pedestals and get us relying on God (2 Cor. 12:7).

- When we have to depend on God to get us through each hour, we really get to know him (2 Cor. 1:9).

- Problems also give us the chance to praise God even when it's hard—it also proves to us the depth or shallowness of our own commitment to him.

- Sometimes sickness serves as God's chastiser to wake us from our sin (Ps. 119:67). This proves to us that he loves us, for every good father disciplines his children (Heb. 12:5–6).

- Sometimes God uses suffering to help us relate to others who are struggling (2 Cor. 1:3–4). And the list goes on.

I sometimes shudder to think where I would be today if I had not broken my neck. I could not see at first why God would possibly allow it—how it could be his will—but I sure understand now. God has gotten so much more glory through my paralysis than through my health. And believe me, you'll never know how rich that makes me feel. If God chooses to heal you in answer to your prayers, that's great—I join you in praising the Lord for his mercy! But if he chooses not to heal you, thank him anyway. You can be sure he has reasons.

Becoming More Like Jesus: The Ultimate Goal of Healing

Christians are careful to pray "in Jesus' name." Especially when it comes to a request for healing. We cling to John 16:23-24:

> "I tell you the truth, my Father will give you whatever you ask in my name. Until now you have not asked for anything in my name. Ask and you will receive, and your joy will be complete."

I asked, in the powerful and wonderful name of Jesus, to be healed. But I never experienced the type of feeling I was looking for… at least not the sort I wanted, like being free of my wheelchair, or at least getting back the use of my hands.

Eventually I learned that praying in Jesus' name includes praying in a way that is consistent with Jesus' character. The life of Christ sets an example for the kinds of requests we might include in our prayers.

There was a time when I thought words like 'suffering' and 'disappointment' shouldn't even be in the Christian's vocabulary. Yet Jesus, my example, was a man of sorrows and acquainted with grief (Isa. 53:3). Hebrews 5:8 says:

> "Although [Jesus] was a son, he learned obedience from what he suffered."

If Jesus suffered affliction and pain, should we expect to be exempt from the same hardships? Our Savior said, "Remember the words I spoke to you: 'No servant is greater than his master'" (John 15:20).

To pray for anything in Jesus' name is to ask God to work in our lives in such a way as to make us more like Christ, giving us qualities that are consistent with the name of Jesus. What could I expect to receive that was consistent with Jesus' name, his character? I prayed for healing, but God gave me something even more precious, something even closer to what his name and character are all about: God gave me a love for his Son. He gave me endurance and perseverance and long-suffering. He gave me trust in the Father's will, and compassion toward others whose afflictions were *far* greater than mine!

Basically, to pray in Jesus' name is to ask to be made *selfless*. I didn't learn to walk, but I learned to wait. I was not given the ability to run, but God gave me rest. God answered my prayer in a way that fully represented the name of Christ.

Will God give you health? Or healing from cancer, dementia, or migraine headaches? Perhaps, yes. But then again, God may give you just what John 16:24 says. He will give—joy, complete joy, *whatever* your circumstances.

God's Priorities

Throughout the Gospels, we see Jesus curing the sick, opening the eyes of the blind, and raising paralyzed people to their feet. These many miracles were Jesus' way of "flashing his credentials" as Messiah; these healings backed up his claim as the Promised One, authenticating his role as Redeemer. Healing was a significant priority for Jesus because it spotlighted him as Christ. This was one purpose behind Christ's healings. But there were more.

Often we hear Christians say that Jesus made clear his intentions by healing everyone who came to him; however, consider insights from Mark 1:32–39. Let's picture this scene in the little town of Capernaum. Jesus was staying at Simon Peter's house and healing all the sick and diseased people who came to him. Very early the next morning, Jesus left the house and went up into the hills to pray. The sun was hardly up and the crowd began to gather with their sick and disabled. "… Simon and his companions went to look for Jesus, and when they found him, they exclaimed: 'Everyone is looking for you!'"

Jesus knew there were hundreds of lame and disabled people looking for him, but rather than go heal them, Jesus simply turned to his disciples and said, "Let's go somewhere else. Let's go to other villages so I can preach in those places *for this is why I have come.*" The announcement of the coming of the Kingdom of God had to occur everywhere!

It's not that Jesus didn't care any longer about the cancer-ridden, or the blind, or the disabled in Capernaum; it's just that their illnesses weren't his main focus. The gospel was! Jesus did not come to make our lives happy, healthy, or free of trouble here and now. He came to deal with sin and all its effects.

True Wholeness

Consider Jesus' priorities in Mark 9:43–48.

- This same Jesus who healed withered hands said, "If your hand causes you to sin, cut it off. It is better for you to enter life maimed than with two hands to go into hell, where the fire never goes out."

- This same Jesus who healed paralyzed legs said, "And if your foot causes you to sin, cut it off. It is better for you to enter life crippled than to have two feet and be thrown into hell."

- And he who healed the eyes of the blind said, "And if your eye causes you to sin, pluck it out. It is better for you to enter the kingdom of God with one eye than to have two eyes and be thrown into hell."

The core of Christ's plan is to rescue us from sin. It seems as though Jesus considers it better for a person to go through life maimed, if it would but keep his hands from reaching for the wrong things, his feet from rushing to the wrong places, and his eyes from desiring the wrong things. This should tell us something about God's priorities: *his priority is our spiritual healing and wholeness.*

"Delight yourself in the Lᴏʀᴅ and he will give you the desires of your heart" (Ps. 37:4).

Doesn't this Scripture guarantee that God will give us the desires of our heart— that is, healing? First, let's consider the desires of God's heart. In a general sense, we can know them, for God's desire is that we be saved, Spirit-filled, sanctified, submissive, and endure suffering. God's Word makes all this clear.

But what about God's *specific* desire for your life? Does his will not include your wheelchair? Or a cane, or pain pills, or a walker? God wants your desires to match up with his, and if you are saved and filled with the Spirit; striving to obey and submissive in suffering… then who is running your wants? God is! And when your delight is completely in the Lord, you truly desire whatever he wants, whether it's a wheelchair or walking.

The End of the Age

One day the Lord Jesus will come back, not as a humble servant, but as a reigning King. When he returns, the last living stone—the last redeemed soul—will be cemented into the kingdom building of which he is the foundation. At that time, he will banish the presence of sin and all its effects. He will complete the kingdom and fulfill every glorious promise. Healing—complete and total—will be ours. Gone will be every disease, banished will be every illness. And death will be no more.

If God should choose not to heal you, can you wait with patience for that coming day? Can you learn the hard lessons that suffering can teach you? It's only "for a little while," as the Bible puts it (1 Peter 1:6). So take courage from Isaiah 35:3–6.

Strengthen the feeble hands, steady the knees that give way; say to those with fearful hearts, 'Be strong, do not fear; your God will come, he will come with vengeance; with divine retribution he will come to save you.' Then the eyes of the blind be opened and the ears of the deaf unstopped. Then will the lame leap like a deer, and the mute tongue shout for joy.

—Isaiah 35:3–6

Until that time, people will continue to live in a fallen world. Nations will keep warring, pollution will increase, people will get sick and die, natural catastrophes will ravage the earth, and yes, people like me will be in wheelchairs. But that's not a bad place to be, for I have discovered that there are more important things in life than walking.

On a scale of one to ten, how often do you ask God to remove a painful situation from your life? On the same scale, how quick are you to tell people about the gospel, the real focus of Jesus' coming? Remember, God saved you to tell others his good news—and your painful situation may be his best platform to showcase that.

There's Healing in Thankfulness

When it began to sink in that my hands and legs would never move again, a friend showed me from Scripture that, like it or not, I was to "give thanks in all circumstances" (2 Thess. 5:18). I wasn't given the option to give thanks when things were going good. The Bible was telling me to *give* thanks, not to "feel thankful." This was a command. *Grit your teeth if you have to, Joni, and give thanks.*

As the months went by, I gave thanks I was able to go to physical therapy. Feeding myself was something else for which I could give thanks. I could sit in my wheelchair all afternoon without losing breath or energy. Soon a miracle occurred. I began to *feel* thankful. It was as though God rewarded me for taking that step of faith in giving thanks. He rewarded me with the emotion of thankfulness. This fresh, bright attitude spurred me on further to give thanks for more things, greater things.

That's when my life began to change and joy and peace filled my days. Was I still in the wheelchair? Yes. But I had made God the desire of my heart, and he had given me a spirit of gratitude. Living with quadriplegia and still smiling? *That's* quite a miracle!

I will give thanks to the LORD
because of his righteousness
and will sing praise to the
name of the LORD Most High.

Psalm 7:17

Books by Joni Eareckson Tada

The topics of fear and hopelessness, depression and suffering, loneliness and worry are issues that author Joni Eareckson Tada can speak to personally. Let Joni tell you her secrets to peace and joy. She knows that God does not take pleasure in seeing you suffer. He has compassion for you and gives you many ways to deal with life's pain so that you can have peace.

Anger: Aim it in the Right Direction

We all have times of anger, disappointment, and frustration. Joni reveals her own struggle with anger after hearing the news that she would never walk again. Find out what she learned from the Bible about how to deal with anger—and get practical tips on how to deal with deep-rooted frustration.

Paperback, 4"x 6", 48 pages,
ISBN 9781628621587

Breaking the Bonds of Fear

Is fear causing you to lose sleep, stress out, and worry? When Joni Eareckson Tada experienced a tragic accident that left her quadriplegic, fear gripped her life. Joni explains the steps she took—and still takes daily—to grow in confidence in the Lord and break the bonds of fear.

Paperback, 4"x 6", 48 pages, ISBN 9781628620481

Gaining a Hopeful Spirit

Finding hope in a tough situation is often easier said than done. But you can experience hope and peace again as you deepen your understanding of who God is. Discover how to place God as the anchor of your life, and find out how to recognize the lies of the enemy that try to prevent you from living a life full of joy and worship.

Paperback, 4"x 6", 48 pages, ISBN 9781628621594

God's Hand in Our Hardship

When you read through the Bible, you can see that God hates suffering. So why doesn't our all-powerful God get rid of suffering? Joni Eareckson Tada tackles the big questions about suffering: How can a gracious and loving God allow anyone to suffer? Why do "good" people have to suffer? What possible good can come through suffering?

Paperback, 4"x 6", 48 pages, ISBN 9781628620474

Making Sense of Suffering

When you're overwhelmed by pain and problems, it's easy to feel helpless, hopeless, and sinking into a whirlpool of self-pity. Joni Eareckson Tada knows about these emotions first hand. Joni shares biblical insights that bring hope and comfort to those who are trying to make sense of their suffering.

Paperback, 4"x 6", 48 pages, ISBN 9781628620467

Prayer: Speaking God's Language

How can we draw closer to God in prayer? How can we "speak God's language"? As Christians grow in the discipline of praying, it becomes clear that there is always more to learn. Joni Eareckson Tada shares personal stories and insights that will help you hone your skill of praying with the Word of God.

Paperback, 4"x 6", 48 pages, ISBN 9781628620498

A Thankful Heart in a World of Hurt

You already know that you have so much to be thankful for, but sometimes it's hard to feel thankful. After living in a wheelchair for over 45 years, Joni Eareckson Tada understands. Weaving together practical insight and Scripture, she tackles key question, such as: How can I really give thanks for all things? and Why should I?

Paperback, 4"x 6", 48 pages, ISBN 9781628621563

Where's My Miracle?

You know that God answers prayers, but what do you do when your situation isn't changing? Joni shows you the right way and the wrong way of coming to the Lord for healing and reveals what the Bible says (and doesn't say) about healing. Find out how to live a life of joy (not anxiety) as you wait upon the Lord.

Paperback, 4"x 6", 48 pages, ISBN 9781628621570

Available at www.aspirepress.com or wherever good Christian books are sold.